ne

The distance between us

Jean Harrison was an accomplished writer whose poems were rewarded with prizes and commendations and achieved placements on prestigious shortlists as well as publication in very many UK literary magazines. Following her debut poetry collection in 2008, Jean had a second volume of poems and two novels published, all by Cinnamon Press, and a pamphlet-sized collection, The Tilt, by Wayleaves Press. Upon graduation from Oxford, Jean qualified as a teacher, a career which took her to Kent, Warwick, Ghana, Leeds, Birmingham, Watford and Exeter, before her retirement to Settle in North Yorkshire. In 2003 Jean was a founder member of Settle Sessions. Based at the Folly, Settle's Museum. This organisation of poets arranges workshops and regular readings where poets with national reputations are invited to perform alongside local poets. Jean died in February 2020 having all but completed the manuscript of this now posthumous collection.

The proceeds from this book will be used to maintain the Contemporary Poetry Library at The Folly, Settle, which was founded by the donation to the Museum of North Craven Life of Jean Harrison's extensive personal collection. Any enquiries about access and suggestions for additions to the collection should be made to the Curator (curator@ncbpt.org.uk). For further information, please see the Museum's website: www.thefolly.org.uk

Reviews of this collection

Jean Harrison's work invites us to slow down and look at the world afresh – in her hands a bird becomes 'an early twentieth century hat / displayed on a stand', buses glide like angels and silence is a light weight fleece. There is often a wry humour at work below the surface of these poems, and always a commitment to careful, concise observations, proving she had a painter's eye and a poet's heart.

Kim Moore, winner, Geoffrey Faber Memorial Prize

These are poems in Jean's characteristic voice and style, full of precise description and telling observation, her thoughts unfolding with everyday eloquence. They show her as someone very much involved with the world, yet also able to stand back and write about it with, to quote Jean herself, 'lines pulled to their full tension'.

Mike Barlow, Managing Editor, Wayleave Press

There should be a 'thunder of hosannas' for this collection from the late Jean Harrison. Some poems have the 'delicacy of a pearl'. Others contain 'an inner boiling, the way the underside of a kettle lid knows the strength of the steam'.

Jennifer Copley, The Barrow Poets

An abundance of inventiveness: particularly intense and detailed observations give us a take on the world that is distinctly Jean's own.

Jane Routh, Smith/Doorstop poet

A curiosity for unusual detail... avoids the obvious and achieves the memorable.

John Killick, Director, Settle Sessions

...confirms Jean Harrison as a talented and convincing writer with extraordinary powers of observation on the human condition

Jan Fortune Managing Editor, Cinnamon Press

An artist's eye for detail... A world where even the mundane is transformed by her vision... A truly original mind.

Jean Stevens, Poet

Also by Jean Harrison

Poetry

Junction Road (Cinnamon Press 2009)
Terrain (Cinnamon Press 2012)
The Tilt (Wayleave Press 2017)

Novels

On a Wandering Planet (Cinnamon Press 2015)
The Fern Hedge (Cinnamon Press 2017)

THE DISTANCE BETWEEN US

Jean Harrison

naked
eye

Naked Eye Publishing

Book design and typesetting by Naked Eye

ISBN: 9781910981122

www.nakedeyepublishing.co.uk

Acknowledgements

The publisher is grateful to Sue Vickerman for editing this manuscript and for writing the Foreword.

Thanks are due to to Mike Barlow and Jane Routh for their editorial support. Thank you also to Jean Stevens and John Killick for their help.

The publisher is also grateful to Managing Editor of Cinnamon Press Jan Fortune and Jane Routh for their thoughtful words about Jean which helped inform the Foreword.

Jean Harrison's family have been very generous in allowing us to publish this collection as a memorial to Jean. The proceeds of the book will be donated to help maintain the Contemporary Poetry Library at The Folly, Settle, founded by the donation to the Museum of North Craven Life of Jean Harrison's extensive personal collection.

THE DISTANCE BETWEEN US

Contents

III A place in the family

IV A place in the world

V A place within

VI Love is a place

VII The last place on earth

FOREWORD

Jean Harrison was an accomplished poet and novelist, willing to take risks with her writing and constantly push boundaries. Jean's poems were rewarded with prizes and commendations, achieving placements on prestigious shortlists as well as publication in very many UK literary magazines. During the last twelve years, Jean's two poetry collections and two novels were published by Cinnamon Press. She had a background in teaching and had worked in Kent, Warwick, Ghana, Leeds, Birmingham, Watford and Exeter over a long career.

Cinnamon Managing Editor Jan Fortune writes, *Jean's work was a testimony to her intellect and humanity. Her first collection,* Junction Road, *sold out and her second,* Terrain, *has very few copies remaining. She came to novel-writing late, but did so with imaginative flair.* On a Wandering Planet *asks huge questions about the folly of the human perspective in an age of environmental degradation, while* The Fern Hedge, *her last novel, mixes conventional narrative and stream of consciousness to explore how Alzheimer's impacts across three generations of a family.*

Poems in *The Tilt*, Jean's last pamphlet (published by Wayleave Press), spanned half a lifetime of teaching in Ghana and are rich in detail and subtle in their critique of colonialism. As Jane Routh, fellow longstanding member of 'The Poetry Business' community of poets, writes, *Jean was a sharp critic in workshops, and of her own work too. I think of her writing as characterised by an extraordinary inventiveness and intense, detailed observation. They're there in 'Woman on the Moon', a poem first published in* The North, *which was shortlisted for the Forward Prize for the Best Single Poem 2004. They're there in her two novels –* On a Wandering Planet *invents a dystopian future in which social dislocation uncannily prefigures much of our present situation.*

Jean was a founder (in 2013) of Settle Sessions for local writers in North Yorkshire, intent on bringing good readings to her adopted home town which engage a wider community than her poet friends. Jean also co-founded Cinnamon Friends to ensure the survival of the press in an era of funding cutbacks.

The esteem in which Jean was held by all of us in her writing world and many in other parts of her life is expressed well by Jan Fortune: *Jean combined linguistic dexterity and rigorous attention to detail in all her writing. And she cared deeply about education, how we live and how we relate. She was feisty and quick-witted and extraordinarily generous. The world has lost a special person as well as a talented author; it was a privilege to work with her and to know her.*

Jean died peacefully at home on 5th April 2020.

Sue Vickerman, August 2020

PART I

A time and a place

Hard luck

All those white muzzled dogs outside in the street
gazing in and no-one's standing up to open the door –
all the people in the room, the man sporting a Man United
shirt, his wife who's doing her nails and their daughter
who's raiding the fridge for ice-cream seem determined
to turn their backs on a gathering of shabby animals,
the yappy terrier with hair falling over its eyes, heavy
jowled labrador, the borzoi with tangled hair and a sad
upward look, the poodle that keeps scratching and needs
to be plonked into a medicated bath, the labrador
limping backwards and forwards trying to see if there's
a fire in there. They huddle together, licking each other,
putting their noses in all the parts of the body that dogs
like to put them. From time to time one shuffles off
towards a lamp-post. They lift pleading eyes towards
every passer-by, one of whom takes one of them, others
mutter they ought to inform the dog warden and he'll
have them put down. A homeless man takes the labrador
Come here, laddie, you'll be a good mate and the Dog
Warden says *let's take them in, disinfect and feed them.*
Should be no problem to re-home them. When it's animals
people will warm to a hard-luck story.

In praise of snails

For their powers as agents of divination
Hesiod says they show the time for harvest
by climbing the cornstalks
and the crown of the Aztec moon-goddess
Tecciztecatl is topped by a snail

for their courtship ritual – rubbing tentacles together,
gently entwining them, launching 'love darts'

for their ability to impress a biped
by walking on one foot

for a water snail displaying its foot
as a blob clung to the pond's surface
walking upside down

for the way they reach out tentacles
with eyes at the end, which they hardly use,
preferring to trust to the nose
that's also out there at the end
to crawl towards their food, using
my garden without my permission.

A friend, a strict gardener
says, *they're a pest. Kill them.*
Drop salt over them.
Quite easy. They'll shrink and dissolve.

No, I say. That's cruel. *Give them a kind death then:*
place bowls of beer on the grass inviting them
to drown in company with drunk companions.
That's degrading to such strange creatures.

Let them have a full life-span
until in the end their empty whorled houses
thin to calcium
that fertilises the soil.

Singing the African Sanctus in Yorkshire

A gentle lift of the conductor's hands
brings us to our feet – no longer strangers
who flocked in from all over,
climbed to this high room, milled round,
flapped off raincoats, settled down –
but suddenly a choir.

Eight spaced drumbeats – then
he releases us to ride our breath
up and down the wide sky of three octaves.

Plainsong's exploding, 'Sanctus, sanctus.'
everything's holy: Egyptian wedding flutes,
Acholi cows, a milking song,
Sufis chanting in the Massa mountains,
the long, undulating flight of the call to prayer.

Under it a thunder of hosannas –
the basses off on their own –
while the rest of us just about hold on
among rattles, drums, ululating voices

and everything rises into the rafters
like rooks circling at dusk, layers of birds
folding and unfolding over trees and fields,
the council houses, the Creamery,
while a few break from the mass,
wheel off towards the hills,
are gathered back.

This place is dedicated to All Birds

that is, to all that deign to reveal
themselves today, that have been
recorded here in the past, that I
may hope to see tomorrow. Better
not hope for too much. A bird
flies in, unexpected as an angel.
That man loaded with cameras
sits, waits, and if an ibis appears
will be raptured up. The woman
in the hide seems absorbed
as in meditation, prepared to wait
on the off-chance a head that's
been pretending to be a reed
may show its real self, she'll
have been granted a view
of a bittern. On the return
to the entrance to the precinct
there are tables where offerings
are made to dunnocks, blue tits,
chaffinches and bullfinches,
and mallard exact respect.

Elegance in North Lancashire

Still in the air, it draws enormous white wings back,
swings wire-thin black legs forwards and down
as if vaulting, lands on the grass.
Five pairs of binoculars and one telescope
cling to the bird as it shapes
into an oval ball of bouncing plumes
quivering on eighteen inches of leg, posing
as if its body were an early twentieth century hat
displayed on a stand,
black straw crowned with curling aigrettes
originally white, dyed sapphire or rose
to shade the glance of imperious eyes

but these watchers keep still,
neither milliners nor hunters,
aware it's only in the last few years
this elegance has been revealed
north of the polders. They lean
their whole selves into their looking

while a long neck uncurls up,
an iris bud of a head tilts down
and, pointing slim feet
it steps into mud, advances into black water,
wades till it's knee-deep, scratches the bottom,
jabs where the mud-cloud rises.

A winter song

The bus travels to Long Preston, Hellifield, Gargrave,
in the misty fields a fine white tracery outlining
every bough up to the slimmest twigs
so they're not blurred ghosts, though less assertive
than the sheen on angel feathers.

I walk with crisp cheeks in a world where white rules.
From time to time a breeze shakes tiny snowflakes
onto the path and I tread on them. They fall too
onto dull-fleeced sheep chomping the frozen grass
the same way as always. Occasionally a bird lands
and the trunks continue to raise an embroidery
soft as a daytime moon onto a grey sky. This isn't
a land of perpetual snow or of melting glaciers.
It's gentle, rhythmic, a distant fable. I hear
a winter song, rising from rime maidens.

In her palm

She loves gardening, has heard
Inverewe's worth a visit - so far north
yet lush and verdant -

takes a trip there, finds on the shore plants
adapted to salt, growing among pebbles
smoothed by the sea's grinding; picks one up,
it's almost warm, and next to it, this fragment
of opaque pale blue glass whose sharp edges
have been rubbed off. Once it was gaudy. Now
it has the delicacy of a pearl. It's not possible
to hold it up into the sunlight, peer into the sparkling
depths of a jewel. It's simply aged, like a good vintage,
except it's this mellow blue, changed
into something rich and rare, a treasure
she might imagine set in a necklace or bracelet
in silver rather than gold

or to leave unset, so from time to time
she can pick it up and feel its
cool warmth in her palm.

Lids

A lid over a ladder that takes workmen
down to a sewer is patterned cast iron.
When it's lifted and flung on the ground
no-one looks at the side that's known
the ferocity of noxious fumes.

People I meet in the street don't look
underneath the smile that hides how
strongly I disagree with what they're
saying, and the boy, whose mates,
to provoke him, call his mother
a slag presents a calm face, turns
away, contains the inner boiling,
the way the underside of a kettle lid
knows the strength of the steam.

Missing

Jump in, the car will take you
all by itself on that route -
Barnet, Southgate, Tottenham,
left past the London Lighthouse,
close to the Hammers' football ground,
round the islanded church at Stratford,
left for Plaistow. Then the long grey wall
of the East London Cemetery and its
implacable wrought iron gates, where the car,
stuck in this interminable jam, seems
to be shivering, as if a deleted programme
were re-installing itself, a ghostly sat-nav
urging *Pass by, go straight ahead,*
as if what's happened can
be over-ridden and you can follow
Star Lane into Desford Road, draw up

and she'll open the door.
Where've you been all this time?
I've missed you.
No. Turn right through those gates.
The car-park's immediately inside.

At the railway station

He hands in his ticket, passes the barrier, strides
through the oncoming travellers and their luggage
with an ease acquired on the narrow quays of Delft
where porters pushed handcarts, staggered under sacks -
compared with that, this moving crowd is nothing - and
comes to a stop, taking in concrete: wall, ceiling, wall -
the interior of a Reformed church isn't as harsh as that;
no wonder these people are restless. He sweeps his eye
over the crowd. It comes to rest on a girl on a blue seat,
head bent forward, dark hair falling over her face, gazing
down into something she holds in her left hand, absorbed,
oblivious. He moves closer, considers the curve
of her back against the seat, the whole body framed
by light through glass that keeps sliding sideways
and flattens her with darkness. He moves round,
studying how the changing shadows bulk her out
till he can peer over her shoulder, view the rectangle
that's gripping her, watch her finger slide
over a surface dark as water where some words
disappear, others rise from its depth. Probably
at this minute he doesn't consciously remember
two other young women, one in a blue dress,
the other in yellow, both with bunched curls
that hang forward while they read, lit by sun
sloping in at a window. Here, strange overhead
strips highlight the crown of her head. He loves
the way she's caught up in a moment that's
taking her, while sitting there, somewhere else.
He puts down his satchel, sets up his easel.
She swings round, glares. He moves to face her,
sweeps off his velvet cap, bows. *Mein Vrou* - they
stare each other up and down. She faces him fiercely,
pale and stiff. He bows again. *Mein Vrou,*
you were so still. It filled me with wonder.

A hungry eye

The visitors frown, the art gallery
sometimes, not always,
stiller as eyes widen –

'What he saw couldn't
have been this, not exactly
this'

but there's something –
intertangled lines creating shapes
that could be oaks
trunks and roots leaning together,
dark and leaning together
framing splashes of sun
caught just the way they fell
on one particular day;
beyond them a range of hills
a local might slowly recognise
as near Porthclais – 'That *is*
what that peak looks like at evening' –
even though strangely re-coloured,
and heaving with
threatening primaeval life –

Welsh landscape 'paraphrased'
by Sutherland's hungry eye
to feed his transforming hand.

A new light

He comes through the war
and in the years that follow
lays enormous rectangular canvases
on the floor, drips fluid alkyd paint,
the kind used on cars, straight from cans
in differing colours, randomly over the surface:

the painting has a life of its own.
I try to let it come through –

Then, leaning forward with straight back and bent knee
spatters it from sticks, knives, trowels, *adding depth*;

later, has his work hoisted onto a wall in the Tate
at a different angle, in a new light
to make us, brief visitors, slow down and look.

The lone and level sands
After Percy Bysshe Shelley

They stand with their backs to us
spaced over the sands, gazing at the sea.
They know the tide must come up and cover them,
that someone may phone for the coastguard,
but today the waters will run back
and leave these salt-encrusted figures,
arms hanging at their sides, waiting
for the moment when they will have to walk
forward and down into the depths
of the element from which the first catfish
scrambled up millennia ago
and draw after them down into the slime
the worldwide mob of Homo Sapiens,
leave the planet to wide-eyed, wandering cattle,
lynxes, natterjack toads, turtles, leeches and fleas,
a world where non-targeted elephants
will show their calves how to tear and trample,
polar bears will sniff new-born ice;
where apes, who never gave up on body-hair
nor took to a strictly upright position or indulged
over-sized ambitions, will go swinging
through millions of square miles of trees.

Acid

The guide's torch searches the roof
for a crack where rain got in,
a little acid in every drop
dissolves minerals into flowstone.
The pale circle moves
over blue-green bumps and curves
that seem to stir like hips and shoulders
in the kind of darkness where people carve gods.

Her ear follows an underground river -
the habitat of blind white fish
who'd survive by nuzzling rock -
and she's blundered along duckboards,
come finally, last in the group,
to stand in a dim space
where she listens to infiltrating groundwater
gathered into a stream

and knows it's been seeping into her for years,
stripping off all that numb-lipped trying
to say, think, do the right thing -

that's when he snaps off the torch,
says: *be quiet, imagine.*
And she thinks, let the place speak.

Falling feathers

A palace with sky for roof that English Heritage
is shoring up. They've fastened a board
to the wall of each room:

hall, where they want me to hear
the laughter of men feasting,
dogs panting on a rush-strewn floor;

kitchen, where a cook is cramming a goose
inside a swan, a chicken inside the goose, a thrush
inside the chicken, a finch inside the thrush

boudoir where a minstrel is plucking a lute
to entertain a countess.

My ear strains for rarer sounds -
sackbut and psaltery - doesn't catch them
and I let the unheard lead me

through a door
into lofty unfurnished rooms
where no princess sleeps to be awakened

or from which a girl fled after opening
Bluebeard's cupboard; nothing there now
but sun-light slanting onto dusty floors.

My footsteps raise no echo while I wander from
one room to another along corridors that keep
expanding. I sense people around me
brushing past, silent as falling feathers.

PART II

A woman's place

In no position

The dark village is haunted by owls
calling from trees only a little darker than
the soot-coloured sky. Crows are nesting
in the treetops, small birds sheltering
in the hedgerows, swifts asleep on the wing.

Humans are mostly in bed, but in one house
a woman sits beside a dying fire, staring at
her shadowy toes. There doesn't seem to be
anything the matter with them. She doesn't need
a chiropodist. It seems she simply needs to stare
at something she can't really see. It's not possible
to know what she's thinking, brooding possibly
on the past, or trying to make her mind up over some
tough decision or dreaming of future happiness though
the way she draws the back of her hand once
or twice across her cheek this last seems unlikely.
She's not counting items on her fingers or writing a list,
simply sitting and thinking while the road outside
is empty. She's in no position to know that in a back
bedroom whose light can't be seen from here
two women are making love.

Tides

It’s true, she thinks, many women have like me
swallowed the moon. Its tides rise and fall in us
thirteen times a year. It rounds inside a womb
and in a child’s face. We walk on the beach, watch
the tides go up and down and know there are times
when vigour flows through us and times when we’re
flat as this sand; that men, who’ve feared us from
the earliest days, changed the name of Astarte,
fertility goddess, to Ashtaroth, abomination.
And then there’s those round faces framed by hijabs.

Handle her carefully

Virginia was born on strike, refused her mother's breast
till she wooed her, later spat a teaspoonful of milk
all over the kitchen so it spattered table, cupboards, floor.
Older, she took against onions, would sit all afternoon
till she had picked out every tiniest shred and arranged them all
round the rim of her plate. At school she sat in the back row
observing every mistake the teacher made in controlling the class,
made a flame spring from a lighter and held it under the nose of a boy
who tried to bully her, struck matches in a haystore after discovering
cigarettes called Lucky Strike. At work, when a foreman sacked a man
without warning, led the ensuing strike. Then took off for the States
and searched the state of Virginia for its Southern possibilities, before
she struck off west into the edge of the desert, where she struck lucky,
learned to pan gold. Then she struck laughter out from deep inside,
couldn't learn to dance the quickstep but danced her own dances
to the rhythm of her own inner music and now she was rich, people
said *she's a bomb of a woman, handle her carefully.*

The population dynamics of fish in some coastal lagoons of Ghana

PhD thesis by Mamaa Entsua Mensah, University of Ghana, 1998

That chapter took me places. You describe journeys
in your own country to the far ends of dirt roads
to meet people you spoke to through an interpreter,
as you leave me your thesis. Two sets of words,
spoken and written, fall together in my mind
to describe how men eye a woman
who climbs out of a 4-wheel drive.

Fishing? You want to know how we fish? Later
you'll call that chapter *The traditional*
management of fishing. They inspect this
curvaceous freak - *Does your husband*
know what you're doing? Next day, warmed more
by beers you've stood them than by learning
their home's *A World Heritage Site,*

they show you how they weight a net and lower it
into what depths and shifting currents; supply
vernacular terms, explain what species of fish
breed here, at what times of year; tell you the goddess
forbids menstruating women to come near the water,
allows no-one to fish on Thursdays. You'll note
an intuitive care for the fish-stocks.

Walk in the lagoon? They hesitate - *Are you clean?*
They wade with you to the sand-bar, demonstrate
how they let in salt water to scour the banks,
and sea-fish to spawn. You'll record
a natural understanding of the ecology.

They take you to sea in boats
forbidden to women, ask for money
to buy nets. Maybe, before you leave,
there’s a moment when side by side together
they and you gaze at a small black beetle floating
on the horizon, inside the three-mile limit,
and silently share the knowledge of what it’s up to.

Just a little squeeze

she said and the light glinted on his glasses
on the far side of the polished desk where all
her statements were displayed as he spoke
severely. She hears his voice as she crunches
her cornflakes, sees his face in the washing-up
water, sits down with a biro and paper – she's
paid the milkman, must top up her mobile, it's
more economical to buy two packets of washing
powder. She still has some cash in the house so
today's the day to acquire that elegant blue skirt
she's been hankering after for weeks and the
carefully cut blouse with heart-shaped neckline
plunging into her cleavage. She'll wear them
next time she faces that icy stare.

A ten year old girl

raises a right leg clothed in black tights
throws rubber under it at a wall
bounce and catch bounce and catch
after ten minutes throws harder
then higher moves back
and throws from there
her mind empty of joys or troubles
bounce and catch bounce and catch
isn't a dance, isn't music, simply
an absorption

a teacher may call her indoors
her mother may call her to dinner -
she's not doing anything useful -
simply giving herself to the rhythm
of a ball against brick.

Looking on

1910, 1920, 1960 – decades of football portrayed
in striped shirts, baggy shorts, hefty folded arms,
impassive Yorkshire faces
on posters headed by three red lines in upper case concerning
the World Cup or Gazza. Paragraphs of small text
get down to Skipton Bulldogs, Skipton Wanderers,
Glusburn Institute Celtic, Addingham Trinity,
Engine Shed, Barnoldswick Mills,
telling who beat whom, who kept sheep on whose pitch,
which match was snowed off, whose socks eaten
by whose goat, which team bravely
fielded seven players and lost 24 nil, what happened one Tuesday
between 'Keighley Police' and 'Skipton Butchers',
who was club secretary for forty years.

The records hoard tallies of cups and medals, don't mention
what it was lured men to spend once-a-week afternoons
on passes, swerves, headers, goals,
Bill's neat footwork, Charlie's sure hands – teamwork and art
I've glimpsed over fences and hedges, a woman looking on
at a game we weren't officially allowed to play till 1970.

There's also a case of boots – the oldest, everyday,
then later studded, with toe-caps, then without,
and the latest, high-tech, supple, green.

Riches

I hate a wind that scrapes across
a wide field, carries the topsoil with it,
leaves it infertile

I shrink from deserts where the sand
reshapes itself daily into shifty dunes
and a traveller needs to know the position
of the sun to find his way to the next oasis

I prefer to talk about a woman
on her knees with a trowel. She
can't be intending to plant flowers
or vegetables or she'd have left
the rich soil, but she's searching
for bones or artefacts, taking off
an eighth of a centimetre at a time
and will call her colleagues to come
running if she chances on riches.

A snowy morning

A table in a warm corner, a large Americano and a cheese sandwich, enlivened by the tang of chutney. Stuffy air pervaded by wallpaper music. From time to time, the door opens, men and women shake themselves, stamp their feet, choose a table, throw off heavy coats, drink, eat cake and talk. Three women lean together over their soup, their voices, backed by a ballet of shoulders and arms, rounded, resonant, wanting the others to listen, each one a rider on a carousel, each feels herself central, the world rotates round her.

A woman in a red coat piles her bags under the table and soon, the scent of tomato soup drifts from her plate. Two girls in high boots tumble in, warm their hands round mugs of black coffee, tuck into chocolate cake, and when they've finished, their voices aren't gently fluid, but breakers running against one another, unco-ordinated, an orchestra tuning up with no concerted rhythm

and now a sudden lull all over the room as if a conductor raised his hands, or an angel passed, and a girl pours into it a dark, cool run of raindrops that flows into a river under trees, ends with a trill that's answered, after a pause, by her friend, leaning forward, placing her hand on the table, in a gentle, hesitant murmur.

An arm round her shoulders

It's there at the corner of my eye, then gone.
There it is again, something active and hidden
and I don't know whether it's afraid of me
and I should be kind

or whether I should be frightened of it,
move on out of range, so I stand,
then decide to move on gently

though there's always the danger it may follow
and take its chance to pounce

but it's always possible
some little creature's lying there twitching
and I could lean over, pick it out of the grasses,
rub its head. If necessary, take it to the vet,

and it might just react to having its cheeks rubbed,
its ears fondled, a hand sweeping the length of its back,
I'd have made a friend.

Maybe it's the same with people. This woman who's backing away
may be in a rush to catch a bus, to finish her shopping or to get home
and put her husband's food on the table

or she may find other people threatening, how they look at her
and make judgements, she can see it in their eyes

and they're right – she's no more than a flicker
down the pavement, too insignificant for anyone to give way to

and when she reaches the Post Office she has to take a deep breath
before she whispers *I'd like to post a parcel* and then
she can't remember her PIN.

Someone ought to put an arm round her, say *You've got it in you,*
you've every right to be here; all these busy people
are covering up their fears.

PART III

A place in the family

Sister

Rows of tall white beds, my eyes
level with mattresses, my mother
above me sitting up in her night-clothes
smiling, and I was supposed to be smiley too -
but why was she there? Why was
the room so big, who were these people
who wanted to take me to another room
and show me something, lead me away
from my mother towards something else
I was supposed to be happy about
when I wanted to stay with her after
she'd not been in our house for more
endless days than I could reckon, but
now they were leading me, pulling me
towards something they called 'sister',
a word that left me struggling
to grasp a reality I would only come to
over years, during which I'd forget
this hall of giants that now, as a visitor,
I rediscover, entering a long white
corridor and feeling myself shrink
as the sense of hidden worlds returns.
I can find my way now, but the smallness
comes back saying, if only I could understand.

Into the dark

In the lightless annexe to the cellar
each makes out the other as a shape,
my sister's head just higher than the table.
We're standing in the place mother waved us to go,
beside invisible shelves of plum and raspberry jam,
bottled gooseberries, eggs in *eisenglas*
though sounds of planes and guns have stopped.
The family would have breathed more easily only
that voice came wailing through the house,
a woman appeared at the top of the steps
red lines running down her chest,
mother and father stared, father ran to the phone,
to his surgery for bandages,
mother waved, *Go*.

We'd come to stand in here beside a crock
into which mother sometimes plunges her hands,
brings out eggs dripping with slime, beside jars
that look almost black when she comes down with a torch
and turn red when she brings them up into daylight.

Today she'd stared up at that lady,
Hadn't turned, had gestured behind her, *Go.*
Now. At once. Don't come out till I tell you.

Ice-cream chimes

From where she's reading
in a deckchair on a hot afternoon
my mother will have heard them instantly
and clenched her teeth. Normally music – if this is music –

slips past me unheard
but this fragment of *Greensleeves*
can run through my head for days
while I wish I could understand
what a tune adds to words –
might this ripple carry
Henry VIII looking at Anne Boleyn,
or any man at his girl, or anyone at someone
who needs coaxing? I'm hesitating
in the shade where the side path
reaches the corner of the house
looking across the grass at my mother

wishing I knew what words
would smooth away chimes
that disfigure a longing
for something more than ice-cream.

My father's skull

My father owns a skull that's stored
in a polished box lined with white satin,
shut with a tiny curving clip

a source of knowledge
he often uses in diagnosis, a relic
he hides at the back of a cupboard.

When he dies I hold it in cupped hands,
imagining a man younger than I'd ever known him,
his fingers moving across it, his head bent over it,

getting to know attachments
of muscles and tendons, shapes of holes
where breath and sight enter the body

feeling the curve the spine makes
to hold up this basket
so an animal can walk upright

handling the bony casket
of a person who'd been the brain inside
and must have gifted it, had hair and eyes

of particular colours, soft lips, a face.
I draw it with a BB pencil, then a second time
to show dark eye sockets, pale cheekbones,
get its lineaments by heart.

The only remedy

Windows that shiver at every draught
let gusts shake them against their frames,
drive the family to crouch by the fireside
while heat vanishes up the chimney, kept in order
at night by shutters, drawn up, bolted, that themselves
rattle as if something out there wants to get in
and there's no knowing what it is, wolf or bomb blast;
so many threats out there, cars with dipped lights
appearing unexpectedly round a corner, a white owl
hunting its prey, and eyes that sometimes let through
something different from what the speaker is saying.

The only remedy – go out, challenge whatever it is which
may be no more than wind carrying with it the Atlantic
or cement dust from a factory five miles away.

Before the ceremony

the dogs had to be shut in the house.

The men stood outside in the sunshine talking and laughing.
Michael remembered he'd forgotten his wallet,
went back in to fetch it.

The dogs got out and leapt about barking. Bob shut them back in.

A three-year-old in a spangled dress ran off up the garden,
found a green beetle she wanted to show her uncles,
was howked off to wash her hands.

The dogs got out and pranced about wagging their tails.

Two generations of brothers and cousins stood among the cars
ribbing each other, Sam went to find out
what had happened to Grandad.

The dogs got out and danced through the flowerbeds.

The old man appeared, a white rose in his button-hole,
two generations of women emerged in exuberant hats,
all the children had polished faces.

The dogs jumped up and pawed their skirts.

They all drove through the lanes to the church
under young leaves and opening blossom
on the only sunny day that April

while the dogs in the quiet house slept.

Bus talk

Thought I was barmy, she said. Oh, I said.
You don't mind me talking? she said. Of
course not, I said and kept my book open.
Wasn't sex, she said. Fifty minutes, I thought,
to Gloucester. Not at my age, she said.
Never too old, I thought, but her? She
could be right. She said, forget, don't you,
what you look like, I mean. I thought – just you,
inside – but didn't say it. And Jim, she said –
that's his name, Jim – has married sons.
Still – ten years younger than me. So
that's barmy, wanting him for my Dad!
Daddy, they used to say. Kids' language.
I wanted him for a *father* – sounds different.
What d'you think? Not the same, is it?
I said maybe not. Depends, I said.
I wanted him and it wasn't sex,
she said. That's different, innit?
Should be, I said. You need to know, I thought.
Felt small, and he *is* taller than me; even so,
he laid his hand on my shoulder and
I felt everything was all right.
Probably was.
Except my wanting him for my father.
What was wrong with that? You didn't tell him?
No! Something like that,
how could you say it?

PART IV

A place in the world

Career project

I set out intending never to return, carrying a rucksack containing basic clothes and a notebook, in well worn walking-boots so I won't waste time on blisters, taking care not to note landmarks, determined not to stop within range of home, where neighbours might spot me and report back they'd seen me going in such or such a direction. I'd choose a path because light fell across it in an unfamiliar way, trees had strange shadows and then there'd be a place where trees thinned and a grassy hill appeared, then a valley with houses like those I left, with inhabitants who'd notice I walked straight through and didn't speak. When I came at last to a place where they spoke an unknown language, though they sold me bread, eggs, milk, something still said this wasn't my stopping point. It might be satisfied by the sight of the sea or it might demand a boat, not to rest on an island – that's too small, too like a prison – but perhaps in the end I might come to a house with a view of the sea and know that was the right place, for the time being at least...

Y promenâd

I follow the lead of
a language I can't speak
to a wind-swept railing

to wet-suited shoulders
blacker than seals
against the shine of a cold sea

to blurs at the north end of the beach
that twist and swing in the gathering dusk,
bend onto a right foot, draw an arm back
and fling, skimming a stone

to dark, shifting facets
of a breaker running sideways

to the thud of descending waves
carried away by wind,
silent gulls banking.

Beyond them all
a quiet curve, edge of the planet
that holds me to it.

Past and present

I've halted between stone and rusty iron
on a flat bridge. Water, though choked,
trickles close underfoot; to my right
a mortared stone wall, to my left
an assemblage of cogs and wheels,
some vertical, some horizontal, cast iron
with interlocking teeth and a handle,
padlocked now, with which one man
raised that huge iron block, the sluice
that drew water from the Ribble
for mill-leat and mill pond. Now the flow's
blocked with *Carex Limosa*, sedge
that loves to have its feet in slime. Sky
shines at head-height through leaves.
On the other side, distanced from me
by a sycamore, a dishevelled willow,
three poplars, all sunlit, a steep green hill
ensures I'm held where past and present
are side by side as one, in a bubble
whose silence seems rooted in time,
where only the four elements make sense:
iron and stone – Earth; a trickle
seeping from river to millpond – Water;
a lightness that rests on my cheeks – Air,
and to my far left, a beech in autumn colours
is blazing down into the ripples.

I've never been a tree-hugger

but have imagined them my friends, confused
by the roughly cylindrical shape of their bodies,
the way they hold out arms, look down
so I'm always a child

sheltering in the warmth of a wood,
running finger-tips into the soft hollows
of ridged oak-bark, caressing beech, feeling
a company gathered around me

like guardians with folded wings, being no wiser
than ancestors who hung scraps of cloth on trees
to beg for healing, poured libations of wine
for permission to cut one down, but now

they've withdrawn into their own business,
converting sap into xylem, light into leaves,
supporting grubs and insects,
welcoming birds,

balancing the weight of branches against
the tilt of a hill, developing twists
that made me think of sinews
when I was a child.

Those that grow on hill-tops bend
before sweeping forces, survive
by being supple, let the winds
comb them, grip the earth, hold on.

I walk in the dark of the shortest day

beside the Ribble which carries peat down
from its source high in the hills and I
barely listen.

A few people pass by with hoods
pulled low over their eyes,
one or two dogs smell me out,

now and then head-lamps
like moving haloes trace
the curve of the bridge.

I stand, breathe in a silence
that has no words and know
day-length will balance on this cusp

at least a week, while the trees sleep.
On the far bank of the river, lit windows
hint at dance music or laughter –

four days till Christmas
and I remember Advent
walks to church

How silently, how silently
we sang, then knelt
with cupped hands

something I
no longer do,
but the mystery remains.

The 'tree pose'

Both sides of the nave, arches,
pillars with clustered columns

tons of stone
like two rows of oaks

branch into a canopy
a still thrust I look for in yoga

one foot planted, the other
right-angled into the groin

hands lifted like leaves toward the sun –
an individual's pose, hermit's, forest-dweller's –

a solitary figure poised between up and down
hoping to be mindless as a tree

but the arches reach towards each other with
more than finger-tips

share out the task
of holding hundreds as one body

at the same time let on
what matters is a wordless

balance
between earth and heaven

Chasm's the word I'd use

for this place where the track sinks
between two steep hills and turns
right-angled under the trees. Sunlight
barely reaches through the leaves.
And there's the rocky path I've got to climb
once more beside the roar of Colden Water,
no longer filling industrial ruins with romance
like Peruvian cities lost in the jungle.

Last time I came it was a game
to balance along broken stone walls,
climb flights of shaped stone slabs.
Today it's not rain that's made them
dark and slippery. I stand,
gaze at the dank mouth of a lime-kiln,
take in that those stone-framed pools
were used for dyeing wool, picture
women bending over them, long hours
of slog and fumes that cut life-spans to thirty
as they blackened bombazine, mourning dress
they'd never afford. I stand pondering how often
my great-grandmother must have worn it
in her ninety comfortable years,
for family, for friends, for this or that acquaintance.

A spider's web looks so frail

One overhead swish of my bush and it's gone.
Naturally I'm not on its scale: this silk thread
pulled from an arachnid's stomach in a pattern
of looped rectangles, each one bigger as the
circle grows, wasn't woven to catch me.
It's all created so a spider can eat, a hidden
hunter with legs of thinnest wire. Although it
looks too dry to digest its prey, the stomach
which exudes that silk has to be nourished.

In autumn I see shawls draped over bushes,
dew strung along their tracery like spangles.
They trap me to stand and gaze and gaze.

Empty suit

Never let your desk face a window. Someone less
focussed than I could be distracted from their Apple
to follow, as it eases out of the station,
one of those steeply sloping white foreheads
towing a body supple as a grass-snake,
catching the eye in brilliant company colours,
capture it picking up speed through the sidings,
racing past rugby pitch, Premier Inn, cemetery,
then fragmented by trees as it sweeps
under the swerve of the hills.

If that weakling had field-glasses he could
pull its lithe form back inside his eyes, grasp
Hull, Bristol, London, destinations where
the sea's insidious tongues
creep up twice a day inside the land,
hang an invitation on the air, slide off

while the empty suit I seem to be
rests a hand on an iron railing, stares
across the river at wet black stones,
watches brown water slip away down
to a mouth that opens into hundreds
of square miles of ocean that thunder
onto the shores of six continents.

PART V

A place within

A tendency to fall into silence

sitting by the window, immersed in my thoughts
while staring into the garden watching jackdaws
gaze down chimney-pots, how their beaks open and shut,
or in a bus watching trees and hills flow past,
letting my eye follow the lines of lynchets, a kestrel hovering,
a pair of crows flapping past, all observed but not heard, not
consciously named, ideas sifting through my mind, silent
as snowflakes, not stored to be thought over later. Anyone
observing might think I was day-dreaming but my mind's
active, recognizing the shapes of this countryside, looking at
farmers struggling to get the hay in a month late because of
the rain; wondering about those clouds rimmed with white
on stormy backgrounds, whether the bus will reach my
destination before I've sorted out how I'm going to handle
the situation I'll find there. Other passengers are chattering.
I exchange greetings and information about where each
is going, the weather, and when all of that has been said
we can let silence pile round us like a lightweight fleece.

One day there will be a slow slide powered by entropy, felt but
unfelt, noticed but ignored, into the silent loss of everything.

Windows at night

10 pm. Rain. No bus. Silent street lined with plate glass,
my only company weightless nymphettes, white-armed,
posed as if they've just touched down on petals, slim enough
to make Twiggy feel fat. Eyeless blocks curving back
from their shoulders suggest heads, for anyone passing to slip on
and dream of a perfect body, but I know I'd be out of place at the party
the girl in a filmy dress is tripping off to, wouldn't like
the man who's taken her friend's breath away and left her with
one hand pressed to her cleavage, one flicked carelessly sideways.

In the daytime, backed by warm lights and moving shapes, while people
not too different from me thrust in and out of automated doors, those lives
might seem one change of clothes away, I'd only need a plastic card.

In the wet dark, a glazed frontage is a proscenium
that shuts me out, unable to run forward, jump onto that stage
and take my pick – but there's tomorrow, and that card

and, still spreading behind me, the dim distance between me
and the man hidden under grimy scarf, hood, gloves, beard
who just now sold me a copy of the Big Issue.

Prayer

It’s a pleasure in December to come in at three thirty,
unwrap herself from her scarf and hang it in the cupboard,
draw the curtains, make a pot of Darjeeling, toast crumpets or
warm old-fashioned English muffins, lay out a white jar of Gentleman’s
Relish, carry the tray to a chair beside the wood-burner.

No point opening the drapes – the days are so short.
She turns off the lamp, wraps flickering light all round her, starts to pray,
Our Father; the General Thanksgiving – *All the blessings of his life*
here in the embracing dark. Touches, on her cheek, the purple mark.

Sits and thinks a long time.

What I'd like to forget

Burrs have stuck in the folds of my scarf.
How did they manage it? Was it when
I leant forward trying to find my glasses or
pulled it aside trying to find that trowel?
Green spots on a pink scarf. Was someone with me?
Did we stand side by side pulling them off? It can't
have been in the garden or we'd have pulled them up,
thrown them in the compost bin, even though we knew
the stalks come away at ground level and leave
the roots in the ground. A very successful plant
that comes swarming back and smothers its neighbours,
a pest that gardeners keep fighting

like burrs in the mind, topics that keep recurring -
being slapped down, or forgetting an appointment
or a family birthday or losing the way
in a town that should be familiar.

Experimenting

She's wrapped a scarf over her eyes,
now feels across the duvet, picks up soft fabric,
rolls and unrolls two crushed tubes joined
at one end, her trousers.

She's lost sight of their blackness, always the first thing
that makes her choose that pair
to team perhaps with a white top labelled 'Regatta'
that she bought picturing a brown hand on a tiller

or a stretchy flowered modal that clung, looked cool
or a red floppy tee-shirt that let her sprawl, blowsy
outdoorsy girl who could challenge the brass of a barmaid or
imitate her friend who bulges out of crimson and doesn't care.

Now, when colour's lost, all that's left is air
between fabric and skin, the brush of cotton.
She smoothes down today's top to shape her
and as she lifts her hands they become solid,
moving over her body, assuring her she's really there
in this dark. But she panics, *I might look totally bizarre.*

When she uncovers her face to visit the town
She'll use other people as mirrors.

Little hops

I read only half understanding, fascinated
by words that swim through me with the ease
of practised arms swinging a body through water,
a head rhythmically turning sideways to breathe
while the swimmer waits for words to rise and
the other person inside criticises, blocks the flow,
says everything I write is rubbish. I can reply, okay
I know you're out to get to me, that what I've got
to say isn't earth-shaking, only my little hops across
the grass, their sound listened to, lines pulled to their
full tension – but yet I dreamt last night I was on a course,
I'd lost my folder of work and was too tired to do anything
but flop. I sat down and cried and the men present said I
was self-indulgent – which was quite right, no-one would ever
want to read my work.

What I say is always more flimsy than the idea hovering
on the edge of my mind. I'm like Plato's seekers for truth
sitting watching shadows of ultimate reality on a wall.

Wiring it up

This phone is black and takes
incoming and outgoing calls

the other beside it is red and when
it rings, someone may say *Quick,*
a fire – or else *a tornado*

or the boss is ringing from the factory floor
everyone down here quick –
a rope broke. Jim took the impact

or it's the Prime Minister –
in one second a cloud will be
mushrooming up.

Red telephones are bad news for humans
and for animals that wander in and out
of contaminated zones.

Was all this pondered by the engineer
who installed the apparatus? More likely he
was simply thinking how to wire it up correctly.

Sharp-edged

Oh yes, I said
should have looked at a hazy sky.
I'd love to, I said
from the clouded depths of my heart.

Oh yes? You said and grew
an enormous clawed shadow.

Of course, I said, no trouble
but when the request came
I couldn't find my keys

though I'd said, I'd love to, gazing
over your shoulder at
a glowing image of myself.

Oh yes? You said in a voice
so sharp-edged
it cut me right down.

Rain

Rain layers the polish on, the rim of the water-butt shines,
paving gleams up; leaves – heart-shaped, bladed or five-fingered –
are shapes cut against increased darkness.
Ivy, fern, lichen, berberis, moss, glow with
the help of more light than seems due from a grey sky

and staring out from within at the forecast's *continuous downpour*
each drop on the pane is glass, magnifying green.

Revelations

This morning's snow fell in huge flakes,
the frozen ground soon snug under a duvet.
Only two forlorn blackbirds hop across.
I shan't go out. The blue and white of snow
no longer entices me. I don't want to throw
myself backwards and create an angel.

They have to carry special news to recipients
only half pleased to receive them. Modern
angels aren't clothed in white, don't have wings.
Messages arrive through other people's mouths
or sudden enlightenments that transform the way
forward. My feet are stuck too firmly to the ground
for me to hear them. Such revelations come to me
clothed in dirty white Samite.

Doing the dishes

I love this frieze of Arts and Crafts peacocks,
tails half-lifted – there's a sense
of the incomplete, a moment most of us
never catch, but the tile-maker did.

Slinky necks stand proud while the birds
eye my kitchen through squared-up vine leaves
that suggest a hidden palace, princess, witch.
Kings used to keep these fairy-tale fowls
as supplementary suitors – it's the way
the male turns its head in front of
a quivering backdrop of eyes, a pose
that could simply mean, *Don't cross me.*

Walk behind, you'll find a rattling fence
of grimy quills, a gaping anus, but
the painter caught the revelation half-way,
back and front not yet contradicting.

Echoes of Ghanaian gongs

In a Devon room I insert a CD, press ‘Play’.
Notes fly and tinkle. A swarm of fireflies
dances over cassava.

Delicate strokes ring,
bell flowers in an ascending scale –
Lily of the valley in a Devon garden.

Slow balances fast, the way leaves
weight the upward run of flowerheads,
or, under the forest canopy,

leathery paddles of cocoyam
shake to a rainy season hammering
and later, drops cling to minute hairs and shine.

Tongueless bells call –
high in a Silk Cotton, among fronds of oil palms,
Bell shrike, Didric cuckoo and Senegal coucal cry, whistle, toll.

Precise blows shiver off metal; banana leaves
held backwards like umbrellas over the heads and shoulders
of bent women stumping down a laterite road – thrum

and as the storm trails off over the trees,
a rusty petrol can, now a water jar
stood under a leak, tings.

In Devon rain drips off the roof.

PART VI

Love is a place

Direction of travel

She chooses a seat facing the way the train's going,
leans back against tough blue nylon upholstery

slowly examines the opposite seat,
pairs of slanting green triangles with black shadow partners

flying away, in diagonal rows –
skeins of geese against broken cloud

hears a continuous brush on the windows,
falls in with a rocking that changes

from clatter to small roll like wheels under a pram
that seems to be moving from bare boards to carpet and back

carrying her to a town where she's come to land
as if she'd had no choice. But she remembers choosing

to follow her friend north and let bare hills and long winters
become familiar, and now she's resting

on an acquired rhythm – Cononley,
Skipton, Hellifield, Settle – allowing vibes

that have been suppressed for a long time
to surface and flow through the pinions

of wild birds headed for breeding grounds
in places that look barren -

Shetland, Faroes, Spitzbergen, Greenland –
each neck stretched in the leader's slipstream.

Here is a room

With thanks to J. Kate's translation of Nikolai Berkov

Here is my room, at least
it's half my room. Which half?
Are the carpet, the furniture,
the air evenly divided?

Here is my room, on the far wall
a drawing of us playing Scrabble
fixed there motionless
as long as the picture survives.

Here is my room, on two walls
water-colours of peonies,
plum blossom, chrysanths
you brought from China

but maybe it's more a matter
of your radio on my table
your books in my bookcase
my bum on your sofa.

Here is a room that's become ours
in a small town where incomers
repeat tales about local characters,
trying to dig themselves in

by knowing other people's roots.
Here is our room where we watch a blackbird
hatched within twenty yards of this spot
tug indigenous worms from the lawn

a space where we've come together
almost by chance it seems
and where could be better
than this box that hangs

like so many others
swinging between past and future
in the whole whirl of the Milky Way
on the curved non-surface of space-time

where two random jigglings
of electrons and neutrons
can sit side by side
and laugh.

Holiday flat in Madeira

From our flat in the Jardim Atlantico Hotel,
the last one in a series perched on the edge
of a hundred foot cliff, all we can see
is sea and sky.

The sun's just set over the water,
it slid down like a coin into a meter
the same red as Barbara's fleece.

I can see her now through the hatch
in the lit kitchen. A wooden spoon
prods the side of a saucepan,
butter paper rustles, and then again
the soft prod of the spoon. Dark gathers
between me in a chair beside the window
and her in the kitchen, unwrapping cheese,
cutting off thin slices for the sauce.
The smell floats down to where I watch
battleship grey clouds in a green sky
and the water sliding dully back
towards the place where the sun was,
the clouds shifting and darkening.

Barbara goes on prodding, gently insistent
as is her way in everything. White hair shines
on the back of her head as she bends it
to snatch the lid off a boiling saucepan,
pour the contents into a colander.

The tiled floor this side of the hatch
is full of shadow now. It's time for me
to stand up and turn on the light.

Album

Faces and places
frozen in a holiday album
as a woman will store eggs
for future joy:

my friend balancing on top of a stile or
cleaning sand from between
her toes against a backdrop
of highland cattle standing in hazy sea.

These were good moments
but what I most remember:

waiting while she inserted toes into her socks,
patted them flat, slowly drew the wool
over instep and heel, then up her leg,
smoothed them yet again;

how we hunkered down
to eat soggy sandwiches
flavoured by mosquitoes
and the heather pricked;

the cliffs above Carsaig arches,
a last day walk in a scotch mist.
A snipe flew out of it;

another walk, high up
between trigpoints -
a view of the paps of Jura
and later of Ben Nevis;

how we tobogganed down over
heather on the seats of our pants.

Autumn flowering

He was lucky, that missionary doctor,
to have this wood to transform, a chance
to under-plant oak, ash and rowan
with rhododendron. Can you imagine him
putting aside his Bible for a stroll round a Chinese garden
selecting specimens to pack up then unwrap here,

re-shape a hillside, disperse a cascading stream
in a calm pond, create scenes like those on scrolls
in the corridor outside your bedroom, the ones
you brought to this country – views hanging from rollers
that, each time you pass them, swing against the wall
and rattle, reminding you where you were born?

This is a good place to be with you.
Let's take hands. They're leathery now – but still –
D'you think he believed in miracles? Look – all round us,
clouds of mauve, magenta, white, and there,
under the bank on the opposite side of the pond
in the gaps between black, floating leaves,
pale yellow petals mirrored in sepia water shine
with the softness of China tea.

They're flowering in late September
though most of their genus
are at their best in spring.

To keep you awake

something small on the feeder – there
in the shadow under the birch, a rapid
drilling –

tiny head
red mask and white scarf, brown shoulders
gaudy yellow wing-stripe

a shocking colour scheme –
almost unnatural –
an artificial bird.

I call softly. You heave off your drowsing
and come swishing across the room
in the mandarin's robe
you bought in Durham Museum – dressing gown
Made in China, brassy rayon brocaded
with trees and pagodas.

The next afternoon the whole flock is dangling
like minute apples on the needle-thin stems
of self-seeded scabious.

Look, goldfinches. Again you leave your chair
and stand beside me open-eyed,
I've never seen them like that before.

All that blue

It’s tempting to bask
gazing up at a blue sky,
be satisfied to think
it’s a solid bowl.

I want to go further,
explore beyond that shining
wrapped round the earth

into the darkness space travellers know,
six hundred miles long

then beyond into radiation from outer space,
quarks and ions, alive with electricity
sparking me on

till I’m caught in the stars, speeding
over the curve of space-time
as we all are

and think of you, my love,
on your own course

like music in another room.

PART VII

The last place on earth

Us then

In those glorious years when the world
had turned its back on war we
swarmed the pavements in striped scarves,
pushed bikes down one way streets,
piled them three deep against railings,
made ourselves chic in old school blouses
dyed pink or emerald, strolled in and out
of colleges where no-one asked where
we were going, revelled in an age of dawning
freedom – we'd been the kids given free rides
on the VE day chairo-planes, had read
how Europe was rebuilding, that India
had won its freedom; as for all those colonies
still waiting for theirs, we were the generation
who'd see they got it, many of us
still classed as children, under twenty-one,
in statu pupillari, referring to ourselves
as 'men' (who wore hairy jackets) and 'women'
(who swanned round in nylons that we mended
with little tin implements bought in the market).
We laughed, we talked, we were sure we'd
put right our parents' mistakes – many of us
first in a family to come here – which showed
the way things were moving into a future
which would be better because
there were clothes to buy without coupons,
cakes without coupons, bread without coupons,
there were crocuses under the lime trees,
we could make toast in our rooms.

The same times

He says he'd like his poems *printed*
in simple type on odd brown paper.
That kind of book used to impress me
and others my age. It's strange –
somehow the young felt the same thing
even if separated by oceans, responding to a sense
of not wanting to make deep marks, a love
of something that lay to hand becoming useful
when it could have been thrown away.

The jacket says he was born in the United States
the same year I was in England. He died
the year we were both fifty-three. This is the first time
I've known he existed. And now his words
call up an understanding so deep
it could have come from initiation into the same
tribal age-group. Certainly we were children
during the same war, students the same years,
when girls went bouncing round in the New Look –

such vivid years, when days glowed
and we threw them away. Later we chained time
to routine, stifled it in cloud, started to say
I've seen it all before, though
this morning the garden was strange
as it is every winter when it snows.

There was a year of deep freeze
when I cut lectures and leant to skate.
I wonder if he did too.

Gaps in the detail

The Angelica bucked and tossed through the night -
Piraeus to Crete, though a metal plaque on the foredeck
announced it had been built on the Clyde, designed for
day trips, Glasgow to Cumrae and back we decided,
students who pictured ourselves launched on an Odyssey
to the land of the Minotaur, plagued by a hostile god, as
the mast swung wildly from side to side on a background
of stars. I sat on deck and ate black olives. My friend
chose to sit on a deckchair all night in the fresh air
but for no reason I can recall I clambered down
a damp ladder to the cabin I shared with four women
in black full-length dresses and their children. I think
the taste of the olives came back and made me nauseous
or it might have been the stink from the toilets, but I was young,
so perhaps I slept. The details have slid away

like this dress pattern that refuses to fit either on the grain of the fabric
or across it, the check cloth shorter than required so that small pieces
have to be squeezed out and fitted into gaps hidden behind the hem.

The Greenwich Meridian

an imaginary line, all extension no breadth,
part of a set that nets the globe, each
so many hours apart from its neighbours,
marking the transit of dawn and sunset
east to west, this one kingpin, the baseline
that once helped colonial slavers to make landfall.

Today, teachers turn the tables, attend instead
to north and south. Schools thousands of miles apart
link up – the *On-The-Line* project – hoping to exorcise
ghosts that too often surface, gigantic and dark,
stalking the tightrope's fragile thread,
one lot muttering 'only fit to be slaves',
the other, 'they still think we're rubbish'.

Here in Accra the teacher waits for the clock's
hands to reach midday – a slippery moment
impossible to pin down exactly till George Airy
came up with *The Airy Transit Device* –
a name that sounds like an edge
for angels to walk on

and now Year 6 in Teshie lean forward
gripping their pens, thinking how to write up their lives
for Year 7 in Ipswich, tongue-tips sliding out.

A right place

Forty years later that book in marbled covers
seemed a relic of another age when I had to
collect it from the office towards the end of
every term and with an ink pen and ruler turned
upside down to prevent blurring rule out a grid
to enter names and results, distinctions in red,
passes in green, fails in black, the whole page
when properly laid out a hard-won piece of art

like the life of the woman who devised the system
whose intelligence, degree, rejection of marriage
back home in England had been black
marks against her but here three thousand
miles away on this African compound
she fitted exactly and saw it was
the same for everyone, that somewhere
there'd be a right place, a proper level,
painful perhaps to find. *Sarah finds*
mathematics hard but never gives up
a comment she liked to write on a report.

Marathon

Suddenly, after an interminable wait
thinking how, with that extra height, I shall
see over walls as from a box in a theatre,
here's the bus that's stretched
the fifteen miles from Lancaster to fifty
visiting every village on the way,
deviating to take in others not so obvious.
It glides like an angel round the corner
by the newsagent, draws in. I climb on board,
sit while it changes its number becoming
a Yorkshire bus instead of a Cumbrian.
The driver gets out for a vape. Once off
there's a roll to its gait, a sound between
a squeak and a rattle, an underneath growl
as it bears me, not with the wings of a dove,
all the way to Skipton. In Long Preston it stops.
No-one gets on. No-one gets off. My destination
retreats by light-years. Once it restarts I turn
and look out, enjoy the brilliance of grass,
trees turning colour, imagine I have a telescope
so I can look through the wrong end
at ash trees, their leaves browning and curling,
horse chestnuts turning gold with disease.
If I really saw them, the lines of my face would
droop like those leaves, I'd be going round
with a face as long as a full-length marathon.

Shock factor

I'd love to ask this girl
stomping towards me along the towpath
hunching her shoulders, face – hidden
under the brim of a base-ball cap –
possibly too thin-skinned to be lifted

who's taking shape for me
gradually upwards from feet lit
as mine once were
by psychedelic socks.

Are hers too
chosen to shake other people
into seeing her? Can she
see me? I fear

I've become only
an old woman she
hopes to shock
by a glow
that springs from her ankles
with the swank of a lion rampant.

Heron

That bird can have no idea how important he is
to the old people round here, though he must notice us
leaning our arms on the rail gazing

as he folds his neck down and
takes up a stance like dead wood while
focusing beyond the tip of his pointed bill
through the water down to a flicker
beside a rock, his eyes not fooled
by the refraction of light.

He can't hear the voices
in the aisles of the supermarket,
the entrance to the Victoria Hall,
among the stalls in the market-place,
won't see grey heads drawing together –

At the bridge yesterday
a frown, *Haven't seen him recently*
relaxes, *Jim says he was up*
at the football ground, re-appears
Worry, don't you? You know
there used to be two.

The next time I spot him, head
hunched into his shoulders, self drawn in,
I see a widower.

My shadow's growing

stretching horribly across the ground.
Everyone's rushing to look. They don't want me,
only my shadow. They're picking it up, folding it,
carrying it off. *Please, please*, but they don't hear.
They can't see me without my reflection. I'm
a lonely wanderer, a ghost of myself –
or someone else? Do ghosts have feelings?
They hang around and haunt. On All Souls Night
I kneel in vigil, pray for forgiveness of all the evil
I have done, and the spirits of all I have loved
rise up to comfort me.

Naked Eye Publishing

A fresh approach

Naked Eye Publishing is an independent not-for-profit micro-press intent on publishing quality poetry and literature, including in translation. We are also developing a 'Potted Theses' series: academic theses rewritten for the general reader.

A particular focus is translation. We aim to take a midwife role in facilitating the translation of works that have until now been disregarded by English-language publishing. We will be happy if we function purely as an initial stepping-stone both for overlooked writers and first-time literary translators.

Each of us at Naked Eye is a volunteer, competent and professional in our work practice, and not intending to make a profit for the press. We see ourselves as part of the revolution in book publishing, embodying the newly levelled playing field, sidestepping the publishing establishment to produce beautiful books at an affordable price with writers gaining maximum benefit from sales.

nakedeyepublishing.co.uk

Lightning Source UK Ltd.
Milton Keynes UK
UKHW021432040621
384935UK00004B/190

9 781910 981122